How To Get Coaching Clients

The 3 Questions That Most Indian Life Coaches Need Answers To

ANIL DAGIA

Copyright © 2017 Anil Dagia

All rights reserved.

ISBN: 9781973237303

DEDICATION

This book is dedicated to my daughter Mili.

CONTENTS

	Acknowledgments	I
1	Two sides of a coin	1
2	3 Questions	9
3	Burn your ships	13
4	What not to do before what you do	21
5	How to be a profitable entrepreneur – My 10 simple rules	27
6	How do you get clients	35
7	How do you find your niche	43
8	How do you decide what to charge	47
9	This is not the end	51
10	ANNEXURE – WORKSHEETS	57

ACKNOWLEDGMENTS

To all my teachers and all my students from whom I have learned a lot.

TWO SIDES OF A COIN

Every truth has two sides; it is as well to look at both before we commit ourselves to either.
~Aesop

As I begin writing this book, I thought it's best to start by introducing myself. I am Anil Dagia. I used to be in the Information Technology (IT) industry for over 22 years. While in the IT industry, I gained a reputation of turning around troubled projects. Then in 2007, I was introduced to the fascinating world of Neuro-Linguistic Programming (NLP). Since that time I became very curious to know more about our thinking process, about how we create change, how we create long-lasting shifts in our experiences that can transform our entire lives & us. I started learning from many different disciplines like mainstream psychology, philosophy, behavioral economics, psycholinguistics, and neuroscience. I even created my own model of transformation called Emotional Fitness Gym®.

I quit my IT profession and I have been in the profession of personal development and transformation for over a decade now. During these 10+ years, I have worked with, trained and coached over 10,000 people across 15 nationalities which includes Americans, Australians, British, Canadians, Dutch, Egyptians, French, German, Spanish, South Africans and much more.

Since the beginning of 2015, I have been conducting life coach certification training under the approval of International Coach Federation, also known as ICF. I have trained 100's of people to get their ICF approved life coach certification. Many of these are experienced coaches who are seeking to add more skills, more training hours, more credentials. Also, many of them are beginner coaches with no experience of life coaching and wish to explore this wonderful profession of coaching & one day transition from their existing career to a successful & fulfilling career of life coaching.

It is from this latter group of people that I am often asked 3 questions in particular.
1) How do I get clients?
2) How do I find my niche?
3) How do I decide what to charge for my services?

Before I proceed further into these questions and their answers, I need to present to you a little background that is crucial to understand the mindset of these people.

We in India are very proud of our culture, values, and traditions. As children, our parents teach us the value of respecting elders. In addition, some of the ways we are expected to demonstrate this respect is to obey what our elders ask of us, without questioning them. In fact, asking questions even out of curiosity is considered a sign of disrespect.

Our parents also teach us about humility, and the way we are expected to show humility and imbibe it in ourselves is by bowing to elders, touching their feet and seeking their blessings.

Moreover, in order to be a good human being, it is not enough to respect just your elders. You are expected to respect anyone who is in a position of authority, be it by nature of being older than you are or by having a bigger job title, bigger position/status in life or any other characteristic that pronounces him or her as "better" than you do.

One more aspect about our cultural values is to be grateful for the food on the table. In addition, One way of demonstrating this gratefulness is to award godlike status to the source of this food. Moreover, a source of food is not just the plants; it is also the provider who enables you to earn money that is to be awarded godlike status. Which means, the company you work for, the boss you work for are to be considered as "Anna data" – literally provider of food and hence must be treated as if they are gods. Another thing about gods is that gods must be appealed to or else you will incur their wrath. Hence, you must do everything possible to appease your gods so that you receive their blessings.

Then there are strongly held beliefs that in order to be a good human being, you have to follow the straight and narrow path and the way you do this is by taking up a job respecting your elders and everyone else who is in a position of authority, treating your boss and your company like they are gods. If you deviate from this, if you think of disobeying your boss, if you are found to dislike your boss and are unhappy with your job, then you are being disrespectful and you are not a good human being. Well, sometimes some grace is allowed for human follies. Therefore, if you are truly unhappy with your job, then the best thing for you to do is find another job and "get settled" – a common phrase used to describe that you are living a life of contentment and being a good human being.

Therefore, the children of India, especially from the middle-class families, which comprise the bulk of the employee population, grow up into adults upholding many of these values and beliefs consciously and these values are perpetuated from one generation to the next. In fact, as adults, these values have been deeply embedded into their subconscious and they are not even aware of how these values act out and ultimately become the source of a lot of unhappiness in their lives.

So let's see how these values act out in their lives. Consider what happens once Sarita, one such good, honest, humble human being with all these values joins a job.

Sarita works diligently and becomes a very dedicated worker. She earns the approval of her bosses and gets rewarded by more responsibilities, maybe a great salary increment and even a promotion. She is immediately considered successful in her society and everyone begins to appreciate how she is upholding the values she was taught. It's all very nice in the beginning but soon, with increasing responsibilities and higher positions, the demands of her job begin to grow exponentially.

However, Sarita is a good human being. So even though she was working 10+ hours, traveling another 2-3 hour and even working from home after that, she doesn't complain. She takes on more and more responsibilities, which burden her even more. When she gets tired and needs leave, her boss pleads to her about how she is such an invaluable person and that the company cannot do without her and she caves in and relents. Instead of taking leave, she now works even weekends.

And mind you, if she was married and has kids, then after returning home, being a good human being and a dutiful wife, she has got to take care of her husband, her in-laws and she has to be a good mother to her children so she has to take care of them.

The story is not much different for Amit. Amit goes through the exact same thing and instead of taking care of his spouse and children, he is a dutiful son. So he must take care of his parents.

Soon all this gets to be too much for both Amit & Sarita. They apply for a vacation. But lo and behold, there is a project emergency and once again, their good human being status is being questioned. Therefore, they sacrifice their vacation because they are good human beings and good human beings do not disobey their gods.

Consider also that since 2008, the global economic climate has been in turmoil. I have seen a steady decline in global employment rates. Part of it has to do with the economic slowdown world over. Part of it has to do with rapid innovation, automation and the onset of completely disruptive business models.

In the 1990's, the major business model at least in the IT industry was to trade time of employees for money. This means that if you wanted to earn more money, you employed more people.

However, consider companies like Airbnb. They have shown phenomenal growth rates but the same has not come from growth in a number of employees. In fact, the same has not come from having an employee base at all. The growth rate was achieved by creating value that does not require employees to create this value. Such business models are overtaking the business world and the employment rates are predicted to go down even further.

Given this kind of business environment, employees in a job no longer feel the security of being "settled". There is a constant threat looming of layoffs and I know that employees in the IT industry here in

India are stressed about when their turn will come (not if their turn will come).

In a growing economy and industry, there were enough rewards for everyone even if you were not the most competent, even if you were a tad incompetent. However, with the changing landscape of business, even competence is no longer a guarantee of job security. This, in turn, breeds insecurities and has led to a rise in "office politics".

But Amit and Sarita were raised to be good humans. So they cannot even imagine what this politics is, let alone indulge in it. So they face the brunt of this office politics and since they are good human beings, they tolerate this without complaints.

Yet, somewhere deep in their consciousness, they search for happiness. They search for that emotion which will allow them to feel connected with themselves and with others. They search for meaning in life, the purpose for their actions, their work and over a period, they find none. They begin to realize how empty their work life is, they do not feel fulfilled to earn this fixed monthly salary.

It is with this background that I have found many people take a liking to life coaching. Life coaching, they believe, is about helping other fellow human beings who are also troubled, about being able to connect with kindred spirits and be of value so that as life coaches they can help their client achieve their results, find happiness and fulfillment. They consider life coaching as a profession, which allows them to be this good human being and earn a livelihood in a manner that is aligned with their values.

3 QUESTIONS

The highest form of human excellence is to question oneself and others. ~Socrates

Since 2015, I have trained 100s of people to get their life coach certification. Many of them are beginner coaches who are now employed in another profession, they are these good human beings upholding the values deeply ingrained within them.

Therefore, they attended my life coach certification training and gained the skills to become a life coach. Also, remember most of their life, they have been an obedient, diligent employee.

Let us go back to Amit, an obedient employee, who was brilliant, does what he is told by the boss to do. He often uses his intelligence to figure out how things are to be done but he always looks for the leadership of what is to be done from his boss.

Moreover, here is Amit, gloriously certified as a life coach and ready to start his practice.

Somewhere within him, he knows that if he could just make it as a life coach, then he would be able to quit his slavery, which he calls employment, and pursue a life of passion, life in which he can ultimately fulfill his dreams. Therefore, he starts sharing this with his near and dear ones, the ones he loves, his family and his friends.

Of course, his family and friend care for him so they do not want him to come to any harm; they are concerned for his life. Therefore, they may be patient with him and encourage him to complete the training, certification. And then they warn him that the best way is to first start earning income from life coaching before he even thinks about changing profession because otherwise he is putting not only his life in danger but he is also jeopardizing the life of his family and he is a good human being, so he cannot do that.

Then, he goes about trying to find clients. Then…?

Suddenly the big question pops up – how does he get clients? He has no idea of how and where to start? Therefore, he starts talking to people, asking them how to get clients.

Along the way, someone advises him that the best way is for him to specialize, have a niche that is unique from everyone else and therefore he will be able to find clients easily. Now the next question pops up – "how do I find my niche".

Some of the ideas he receives and implements get him that occasional client or 2. Then the 3rd question pops up, usually because the potential client asks it – how much will you charge?

There he is now stuck with these 3 questions and no way to find a conclusive answer.

Most often, Amit like many others in his situation is unable to find these answers and within 6 to 9 months gives up the idea of pursuing life coaching as a profession. Not only does he give up on life coaching, but also he resigns himself to his fate where he has to suffer the drudgery of employment despite being terribly unhappy. He gives up on all his dreams, never to be talked about again.

Since the time I have been training people to become life coaches, I have seen many Amits and Saritas. It's the same story with many people. Maybe this is your story as well.

BURN YOUR SHIPS

Consider that people are like tea bags. They don't know their own strength until they get into hot water. ~Martin Luther King Jr.

I have also had occasional students like Dinesh and Sambhav. Dinesh and Sambhav were exactly like Amit and Sarita. However, they were determined. For them, their dream had become far more valuable than anything else in their life. Therefore, they persisted and found their way. Moreover, it did not take them long to make it out on their own. They took a leap of faith and quit their jobs even before they had their first client. So how did they manage?

Napoleon Hill in his book Think and Grow Rich describes a warrior who has to send his soldiers against a formidable enemy whose men greatly outnumbered his own. He took a decision, which insured the success of his men. Once he landed on the shores of this country along with his men, he ordered the soldiers to burn all his ships. Addressing his men before the first battle, he said, "You see the boats going up in smoke. That means that we cannot leave these shores alive unless we win! We now have no choice—we win, or we perish!"

They won.

Often we do not realize our own power of what we can do until we are faced with challenges so big that we are forced to grow. When you truly burn your ships, it's almost like magic. All your energy, your entire conscious mind, AND your sub-conscious mind obsess with how to succeed.

Dinesh and Sambhav burned their ships. They put themselves in the uncomfortable position of not having a job, not having the security of a fixed monthly income. The only option left for them was either to earn through the pursuit of their dreams or to die trying. Within less than a year, both Dinesh and Sambhav had earned upwards of ten lakh rupees, which is more than enough to sustain the livelihood of their families without sacrificing their lifestyle of comfort, which they were used to.

This was just their first year into their own venture and they had worked lesser number of days than on their job, they had the freedom to wake up and work when they wanted, freedom to work with whom they wanted and most importantly they did work in which they could pour their heart and soul, something that they loved. Despite all this, I know Dinesh and Sambhav to still be the same good human beings they were raised to be by their parents.

My own story is no different. I was raised to be a good human being. I took my job very seriously and was the most dedicated and diligent worker, putting more hours than anyone, sacrificing more than anyone else does in the office. It just got to be a bit too much at one point in time and I was very unhappy not because I didn't like my work, but because there was always this conflict between me – to be either a good human being as per the values taught by my parents and what society expects of me or to pursue my dreams and happiness and risk being considered selfish, shameful and an embarrassment. However, my dreams were bigger than my fears. So I quit anyway.

Unlike Amit, I didn't have the support of my family. My friends or those whom I thought were very close friends, all deserted me. I was subjected to massive ridicule for being foolish and getting my head into something, they believed I couldn't handle. They were right. I had no prior experience of being on my own. Nevertheless, I had a burning desire and I was willing to learn. I even asked them to teach me since they knew. Nobody came forward to teach me.

I was subjected to emotional guilt for being selfish and thinking only of myself and not of my family. In addition, all along, my thoughts were that if I am unhappy, how can I give happiness to my family, to my daughter who means more than anything else to me? In order for me to be a source of happiness, I have to have happiness within me.

In my situation, I had no support system. No family, no friends to fall back on, no one to guide me. I had to figure things out the hard way. By making mistakes and learning from them.

Today, I am proud of what I have accomplished.

I quit my lucrative, comfortable & high paying, successful career of IT in 2011 to get into the profession of training and coaching. Since then, I have had the good fortune of being able to train and coach over 10,000 people from across 15 nations. I became one of the top NLP trainers in the world after I gained a global trendsetter status when I became the 1st NLP trainer in the world to get an NLP certification training to be approved by International Coach Federation (ICF) for life coach certification training.

Financially, I have reached a stage where my income consistently exceeds what I used to get from my job. After quitting my employment, I realized that it is not only possible, but it's very fulfilling to earn an income of several 10s of lakhs along with the freedom to choose when you work, whom you work with, what you work on as well as choose your own purpose to pursue with your work.

Moreover, just in case I had not made it clear, I had no prior experience of setting up or running a business. I used to hate the very notion of selling as a profession. I still do not like "selling".

My point is simple if you have the burning desire strong enough stoked by the fumes of the ships you burned, then making this transition is not only possible but you find that your life becomes much more rewarding and you are filled with happiness and love within yourself. You become a happy and loving person. The conflict within you between being happy and being a good human being disappears.

That reward cannot be measured by any amount of money in the world.

By 2016, I had already achieved substantial success in my business. Yet I didn't consider what I was doing as a business. To me, it felt more like self-employment. I was hungry for more. I was ready for more, so I enrolled for Business Mastery program conducted by Tony Robbins.

My logic was plain and simple. Tony Robbins is the most successful person who emerged from the field of NLP. His companies are worth around US$ 5 billion. His own personal net worth is about US$ 0.5 billion. He owns an island. He has built a resort on that island which I have heard is by invitation only. Tony Robbins' financial success is probably far more than the collective financial success of all the industry of NLP put together in the rest of the world (not that any statistical data is available to confirm it).

Hence, I decided that if I wanted to learn what running a business is truly about, I would learn it from Tony. That is how I found myself in Amsterdam in June of 2017 for 5 days of super packed learning which changed my life forever.

There were many takeaways for me from that training. One of them was to love my clients and not my products/services. I needed to listen to the voice of my clients and create so much value for them that no one else can and no one else does.

Moreover, that's when it really struck me. I had indeed been in love with my products, my training and in doing so I was missing the most important aspect – the 3 questions that my students were asking. They needed these answers. Many Amits & Saritas need this answer. Many, who like me, have nowhere to seek answers from and I was in a unique position of being able to provide the support, which I had never received. For me, it has been trial by fire. It need not be the same for my students.

That is how I got around to formulating answers to these questions and that is how I started thinking of writing this book.

At the outset, this book may appear to be very basic steps for a beginner to take. This book is about getting your basics right. It's about making sure that the right type of soil has been used to plant the seed. You have to nurture the seed until it sprouts into a sapling & then grows into a plant/tree that bears fruit over a period. After you get your basics right, you have to put in the hard work to start getting your results & these results may take some time but you will get them for sure.

I have found that even though I have been training professionally for more than 7 years now, I benefit hugely from going back to relearn all my basics from scratch every now and then, so even if you already have some experience with running your own business, you will still derive value from it.

Moreover, even though this book is primarily for those who want to transition to the coaching profession; the basic principles apply to all businesses. So even if you are in a business other than coaching and training, you will still benefit from this book.

WHAT NOT TO DO BEFORE WHAT YOU NEED TO DO

Deciding what not to do is as important as deciding what to do. ~Steve Jobs

Before I answer the three questions of what to do to get clients, find your niche and decide your charges, it is important for you to know what not to do. In my experience of working with and training people wanting to become life coaches, I have met many life coaches, and I found that some of them make fatal mistakes, 3 fatal mistakes to be precise.

It is crucial that you learn from other's mistakes and ensure you do not repeat them because doing so would mean that your chances of becoming a successful life coach would be over even before you begin.

1st Deadly mistake life coaches make.
In India, the word coaching is synonymous with

academic coaching to score better in competitive academic exams. Your potential client has no understanding of what life coaching or executive coaching is all about. Add to this the fact that life coaching is an abstract subject and there isn't anything else tangible that you can relate coaching with to facilitate an understanding of it.

This is where most life coaches make their biggest mistake. In order to explain, they either give a complicated definition for the subject or use other even more abstract concepts/terms to explain.

Result being - your potential client still hasn't understood anything. At best, they will wish you the best in your endeavors & at worst; they will make up their mind that you are making up bullshit.

This ensures that you are erasing your business even before you begin writing because the biggest target segment for your offering is the population who knows nothing about your field. If you can handle your introduction well, then you can be the first person to get business from them & then retain your client base with good work.

In order for you to explain, what your subject is all about, you have to ensure the following:
a) Make it tangible for them
b) Make it tangible in a context, which is relevant to them.

During my life coach certification training, I teach people how to make an abstract concept/topic tangible for your potential client and thereby ensure that you can be the first to catch their attention.

2nd Fatal mistake life coaches make.

The 2nd fatal mistake Life Coaches make is - NOT charging for their services.

This is not the same as offering a free sample. Every profession has its own version of FREE samples.

However, Life Coaches refuse to quote a price for their services. And there are several versions of this phenomena which includes but is not limited to - refusing to ask for anything in lieu of the services provided, leaving it up to the "client" to decide the payment, asking the "client" to give a "gift" etc.

There are 3 reasons for this & often more than 1 of these reasons are at play:
1) They do not have confidence in the value of their services
2) Even if they had the confidence or manage to build it, they equate their work with being kind & empathetic towards others & hence - "how can I charge a price for being kind? If I charge a price for being kind then, am I being selfish?"
3) When push comes to shove & their survival may be at stake & they finally muster up the courage to charge for their services - they find their service to be too abstract and intangible and hence they do not know how to come up with a price for their services.

Given these 3 levels of complex human emotions

& decision-making process, they may soon reach a stage where they decide to quit this profession.

Not charging a "FAIR" monetary price for your services directly destroys any prospect of business you might have had. The discerning client, who is willing to pay for the services, finds this as a reason to become suspicious of the quality of service you claim to render & may find you downright unprofessional.

It's a profession - Be "Professional" about it.

3rd Lethal mistake life coaches make.

The 3rd mistake made by life coaches, which is lethal for their credibility - is to make an unsolicited pitch for their services or pop up the benefits of their services during unrelated conversations - unsolicited pitches.

Life coaches who have already been making the above two mistakes find themselves in situations where business is not easy to come by. This then leads them to desperation & in that state they will pitch their offerings anywhere, everywhere, all the time.

Take for example a very simple conversation that had been started in a WhatsApp group - one of the trainers brought up a discussion regarding the usage of "Sir/Madam culture v/s First name basis culture".

Several people provided their opinions & the discussion & debate was quite lively & healthy.

Then jumped in an NLP coach into the discussion with a pitch of how NLP can help & that the initiator of the discussion needs to undergo NLP coaching!

Really? Was there any need to pitch for NLP? Couldn't you just have joined the conversation and contributed your comments like everyone else?

A modified version of this mistake is blabbering out jargon from your field of study during conversations, which have nothing to do with your services & to people who have no interest in your field.

Any unsolicited pitch during unrelated conversations or blabbering out jargon is not only ignored but it reflects poorly on your credibility. Discerning clients recognize this as a sign of desperation. If you are seen to be making such unsolicited pitches, you will rapidly lose credibility, the word will spread, and it would become even more difficult to generate any business.

Given these 3 mistakes that many beginner coaches make, it is no wonder that so many life coaches do not survive long in this business. The mortality rates in this business are extremely high & the average life expectancy of this business is between 6 - 12 months. Some may survive longer but only manage to crawl along for appearance's sake because they are too vain to admit that it's no longer viable for them.

The 3 key learning to ensure that you avoid making

these mistakes are:
a) Learn your subject from a proven expert who can teach stuff to you in a simple & effective manner that helps you apply it in your everyday situations
b) Learn it in a way that makes it tangible to you & hence enabling you to make it tangible for others
c) Learn to be a professional. This includes knowing what to sell when.

HOW TO BE A PROFITABLE ENTREPRENEUR – MY 10 SIMPLE RULES

It is important for young entrepreneurs to be adequately self-aware to know what they do not know.~Mark Zuckerberg

Year after year as I finalize my books of accounts, I realized that I have been intuitively following some principles that ensure profitability of my business. Those of you, who stand at the crossroads, would do well to become aware of these principles.

1) Go out there and do it.
I know too many wannabe coaches and trainers who just keep thinking up ideas of what they could do. They even go and are trained and certified. However, they never get off the ground.

If you want to fly high, you first need to take off and lift off the ground.

Go out there and announce your services.

2) Publicly announce your services.

I know some people who never make a public announcement of their services or themselves so that their competitors don't get to know much.

Guess what. NEITHER DO YOUR CLIENTS!

Go out there PROCLAIM YOURSELF & YOUR OFFERING.

3) Do your own push-ups.

If you are a start-up or a relatively new into business, you might have a temptation to tie up with companies that offer to market your services for you.

Chances are they will ask you to market their brand name and their services using your own resources - time, effort and money.

RUN LIKE HELL away from them!

This will not only consume your valuable resources (with no returns), it will also divert your focus from your business.

Forget those firms that promise you to market your services for you.

4) Avoid the web of business networking dinners/meetings.

Work hard & spend your time meeting your

potential customers.

What makes you think that you will be able to get business from these networking dinners/meetings?

The people who come to these meetings are there to sell their offerings and have no interest in buying your offering.

Go to forums where you can directly meet your target clients. This will yield business more effectively and efficiently.

5) Driving your car? Don't expect help from the driver of another car.

If you are a start-up, you might think that you could ask and receive help from others in the same business. After all, they had started up some time. They would know the pain and struggle of being a start-up. They would want to help others in the same situation, wouldn't they?

Ask yourself, can the driver of another help you with your driving even if they wanted to?

Others are busy with their own business and marketing of the same.

Your best bet is to spread your own word and don't expect anything from others.

Help will come in its own form, which you may not even have imagined.

6) What is your price?

If you are a start-up, you might have wondered what the right price for your offering is. You might even have thought that pricing it low would help you gain an easy entry into the market.

BAD IDEA!

The lower you price yourself, the more you devalue your offering. A lower price will not attract true seekers of knowledge. It will only attract those who are skeptical of your skills and/or those who are skeptical about seeking the knowledge you have to offer.

Secondly, competing on price is a sure way to head yourself to losses since someone else can easily come and down-price you.

Instead, find out what the best in your league of offerings charge. Then price yourself slightly higher than those.

Then offer something extra which they do not offer!!

Even if you offer 1 extra which they don't offer - you make yourself stand out better than them.

7) Dying of thirst and finding salt water.

Would you drink salt water and quench your thirst if you were stranded on a desert and dying to have a drop of water? Moreover, even if you did, will it quench your thirst or will it make you thirstier?

Do not ever make the mistake of taking up an assignment, which is not fit for your strengths or those, which you are not best suited for.

It is better to pass up the opportunity to someone else and earn the goodwill.

8) Raise your bar.
Invest in yourself. Reinvent yourself on a regular basis. Invest in obtaining yourself accreditation and professional memberships in your own field.

It is one thing to be good in your knowledge and content. It is a very different level of the game to invest in and publicly announce your commitment to your field and a professional accreditation and membership will do exactly that.

The market is filled with products. Only a few commit themselves to internationally accepted standards.

Commit yourself to internationally accepted standards. Learn from someone who demonstrates the same commitment.

9) Circle of life.
What goes around comes around.

Did you choose to go to the cheapest course? Did you search for ways and means to extract discounts? Were you always looking for how you can get things free, the cheapest deal?

If you were the one who made your choices simply because of the price, you pay without any consideration for the value offered, then that is the exact type of clients you will get.

This is not based on some spiritual karma theory. This is based on a factual premise that if you have not invested based on value; your mind is not tuned towards value. Hence, your entire approach towards marketing your product will be based on cost (not value). This will directly attract inquiries from people who are looking for a cheap bargain.

10) Start with the why.
Start your venture by identifying why you want to be in that venture and by why, I do not mean revenues & profits. Those are the outcome of your venture.

Your why has to be the purpose you want fulfilled by your venture. Your why has to be about your beliefs, your values, your sense of your vision for not just yourself but for your clients and the community that you will build with them. Your why and your purpose is what you stand for!

Identify your purpose and then always stay connected with this "Why", with this intent, with this belief, with your values. This will automatically direct your actions towards attracting clients who value the same thing, who believe in what you believe in, and this will directly impact your sales process. If they already value what you value and believe in what you believe in - then it is just a matter of time.

HOW DO YOU GET CLIENTS?

Sometimes the questions are complicated and the answers are simple. ~Dr. Seuss

It is time I answered the first question - How do you get clients?

Before I begin, let me reiterate that the answers to these questions are about getting your basics rights. These are the very principles that many of my students have used and already earned 10s of lakhs in income within less than a years' time.

These are the very principles by which someone like me, who had never sold anything, and who absolutely hated the notion of selling, was able to apply it to my business and have been successfully earning a lot more than what I used to earn in my salaried job and the best part is - it never feels like I am selling anything to anyone.

The point I am making is that you don't need to be

an experienced salesperson. You don't need to even like the notion of selling. All you need to do is just get your basics right.

All right, so let's begin with the answer to the 1st question - how do I get clients?

Surprisingly enough, the answer to this question is a series of questions, 5 sets of questions to be precise.

Questions that answer a question, what do you mean?

Let me explain. Have you ever gone to a grocery shop to get something for the house? Let's say you wanted to get butter. What did you do? You knew where you would get butter. You went there. You knew exactly what that packet of butter looks like, what size is it, what color is the packaging. You even knew where in the store it is kept, so you went directly to that place & got yourself some - "butter".

Anytime you have been consistently successful in "getting something", you would realize that you were very clear about this thing that you wanted to get. You had a very rich set of mental images for it, you knew many details about it, and your notion about that thing was very sharp, unmistakably precise.

So let's get back to your question - How do you get clients? You know what you want - "clients", but ask yourself what kind of mental images you have about "clients". Do you have vivid details or is it just some abstract notion of people who would pay you money for something called "coaching"? There is a high chance that you have just a vague notion of this term "clients".

The very first basic that you need to get right is to create a very precise understanding of this term - "clients". Your understanding must be so clear that if you are in a group of 100s of people, you should be able to pick out exactly who would be your client and in order to do this; you need to ask yourself these 5 sets of questions & answer them.

The 1st set of questions

Whom do you want as your client? Is it any person? On the other hand, is it a specific group of people (hint – it needs to be a specific group of people)? Is the group based on their profession, their industry, their stage in life, their age, or some other characteristic?

Once you know whom you want as a client, what group they belong to, it becomes easy for you to find out where you can get to meet them, interact with them, connect with them. With that, you have already overcome your 1st hurdle of - where do you find your clients.

Note that you could have multiple groups of people whom you want as your client. Therefore, you need not restrict yourself to one group, but you do need to get the details of each group individually.

Once you have identified the group of people whom you would like as your clients and started interacting with them, it is time to ask the 2nd set of questions.

The 2nd set of questions
What are their dreams, their aspirations? What do they want their life to be like? What motivates them? What gives them energy, their drive?

Once you get to meet with your potential clients, interact with them, you have to put in the next bit of work on your part - find out what makes them tick. Connect with them such that they open up about their wants, needs, desires & dreams.

Now, if you have attended my certification programs, you know you have already learned some very powerful skills with which you can instantly establish a deep rapport that gets them to feel powerfully connected with you.

Knowing about their dreams & aspirations is good, but in my experience, I have found that people will take a lot more decisive action to move away from some unpleasantness than they would to gain some pleasure, so it helps to find out what challenges, what problems your potential client is facing. What fuels their anxiety, nervousness, worries.

The 3rd set of questions
What are their challenges? What problems do they face on a recurring basis? What are their fears, their worries?

Because finding out this information in and of

itself is an indicator, of how much this person has started trusting you. People usually feel uncomfortable to admit even to themselves about these things and if they have opened up to you about this, it means they feel that much comfortable to share with you what they hesitate to admit to themselves.

Wouldn't you say that you have already started coaching this person?

Besides, getting to know what someone else is going through, being able to empathize with them, allows you to connect heart to heart and that is a reward in itself, isn't it?

Here is the thing. At this stage, you have already connected deeply with your potential client, they have shared their dreams with you, and they have even opened up about their deepest fears.

The 4th set of questions

How do your services contribute towards the fulfillment of their dreams? How do your services help them overcome the problems that they face?

While you have been, finding out what your potential client aspires for and what are their fears, you would have already begun to form an understanding of what kind of insights you can help your client gain.

Well, it's quite likely that just during the process of interacting with them, asking questions, you might have already enabled them to work out their solution, their strategy to move forward.

This is where you become clear of how your service adds value to your potential client.

Now, this is where the crux of the matter is. You MUST make it a point to communicate this to them. Because if you don't, then forget about getting a client, forget about getting ANY client.

You HAVE TO communicate what you do, what service you provide & how that adds value to this potential client and possibly other potential clients in a similar situation.

That is how you begin the process to get clients.

5th set of questions

How willing your potential clients are to do something about their goals and limitations? Are they willing to seek help? Are they willing to pay for this help? Do they want to opt into your services and pay for the value your services provide?

Because let's face it, there are individuals who either do not want to take steps towards the life that they desire or at the least not interested in seeking help from anyone else nor pay for those services.

Therefore, you may have done your homework well & be convinced that your services will serve the needs of a particular individual. Even they may be convinced that your services do provide value.

However, if she or he is unwilling to do anything to seek your services, to pay for your services - then there's no point in pushing down that path.

The point is that coaching is a profession. Moreover, in any profession, you need to ultimately transact your product/service in exchange for money. For that, you need to know who the buyer is, you need to know what does the buyer want; you need to know whether a person will buy.

These 5 sets of questions are the basics. You MUST get these basics right.

Also, remember, as you start answering these questions, you may become aware of even more questions. That is part of the process of seeking to understand your client and it is normal to have more questions.

As you begin to apply these principles, you might benefit to use the worksheets provided to you in the ANNEXURE.

HOW DO YOU FIND YOUR NICHE?

You have your way, I have my way. As for the correct right way, and the only way, it does not exist.~Friedrich Nietzsche

Let us look at the next question - How do you find your niche?

Before I answer this question, let us understand what a niche is. Niche as per the dictionary means - "denoting or relating to products, services, or interests that appeal to a small, specialized section of the population". Simply put - it is an area of specialization.

Why is it better to specialize? It is always better to specialize because firstly, you have a defined set of people who would be your potential clients and hence it is easier to know about their situation & plan a variety of services for them. Second, as you gain more experience, you become an expert in your area of specialization, your niche and people begin to view you as an expert.

So how do you find your niche?

For this, ask yourself if a particular area of coaching or a particular group of people appeals to you so deeply that you would focus only on that area and no other - let's say for example relationship coaching for couples or let's say coaching troubled teenagers as a group.

If you are certain that this area appeals to you strongly, then you already know what your niche is. You may not know yet how much income you might be able to earn from specializing in this area and that is alright. There is no way of knowing that upfront anyways even if you did not choose any niche. Just because you focus on one area does not prevent you from taking up coaching in other areas occasionally.

If you still have this question of how do you find your niche, chances are that you really haven't found any area that you can be passionate about and even that's ok. It's ok to take time, build experience and then decide what your niche will be.

Moreover, how do you do that? You do that by first focusing on building your coaching experience and at some point in time go through the list of clients you have had phenomenal success with and notice if there's any pattern. The pattern could be a group of people; pattern could be a result area for the client.

Once you begin to notice a pattern, you can then start focusing on it while checking within yourself if that's what really connects with your passion, motivates you and drives you. As soon as you find one that appeals to your heart - you know that's your niche.

What if you don't recognize any pattern? What if the pattern you recognize does not appeal to your heart?

Even that's OK.

Just remember that being a generalist rather than a specialist has its own advantages. You have a broader & diverse base of people who can be your clients. That means a steady flow of business for you.

If you haven't found your passion yet, then just start coaching, get clients, work with them & soon enough you will develop your niche.

Simple - isn't it? Yes & no. There is, of course, a lot more to it once you get started. The key is to get started first and starting is very simple.

So continue on with your good work, start getting clients, start working with them.

Once again, refer to the worksheets provided to you in the ANNEXURE to help you as you begin to apply these principles.

HOW DO YOU DECIDE WHAT TO CHARGE?

Price is what you pay. Value is what you get.
~Warren Buffet

How do you decide what to charge for your services?

Unlike consumables, pricing for coaching services is not a function of demand and supply. If you get into that trap, you will find yourself charging low fees and there will always be someone willing to charge even lower.

Besides, what are you communicating when you quote low prices? That your services are worth only that much? If that is the worth you put on your services, how does it measure up in your client's mind? Think about it!

In order to decide about your pricing, you need to consider 4 dimensions:

Dimension 1

What is it worth for your client to get their results, overcome their challenge? How much value do they attach to their own results?

You need to know what value is perceived by your client to get their results. If your client does not consider their results worthwhile, ask yourself whether you want to work with such a client? Because your client will invest only that, much time & effort as the amount of value they attach to it & if that's not a lot, what are the chances they will really, go all out for their own growth?

Dimension 2

Their certainty - how certain are they that they will get their results? How certain are they about your capabilities to help them achieve their results or their need to use your services for it?

Let's say that your client considers it hugely worthwhile to work towards their results. However, if they have a very low certainty of achieving this result then their efforts would be quite half-hearted, won't they?

Given this, you might then think that it is better to have a client who is more certain of achieving their results. Nevertheless, here is an interesting paradox. If they strongly believe that they can achieve their results, then with that level of certainty, they won't see a need for your services.

Therefore, your client is going to be someone who

has enough certainty to put in his or her effort, at the same time uncertain enough to seek help.

Then the next question is - how certain are they of your capabilities to help them achieve their result? This is where you need to have your story ready, one that convinces them beyond any doubt about your capabilities.

If you are just starting out as a coach, then this is where you might not yet have enough success stories. I will repeat what I said previously - the key is to get started first and starting is very simple.

Dimension 3

How much would you earn if you put the same time on another revenue earning or income-generating work of yours?

You have to be very clear of how much you can earn from the amount of time you put into something. You need to earn at least that much from the time you spend with your client for your services if not more.

This is where many beginner coaches face a challenge because beginner coaches do not have too many clients and not much income from coaching to count for. Remember that as a beginner coach, you are most likely in an existing profession different from the profession of coaching. I suggest you calculate your hourly income from your current profession. That's a minimum you must consider charging per session of 1 hour for your coaching services, if not more.

Dimension 4

How certain are you of earning the income from other revenue earning/income generating projects?

Here is the thing. If you are absolutely certain that you can earn a lot more from your other projects, then you would not settle for anything less than the same from your clients - would you?

Beginner coaches do not have this certainty because they may not have so many income earning projects. Here again, you know for a certain how much income you generate from your current profession. That is a given. Hence, your certainty level is high. You must charge at least that much if not more.

These are the 4 dimensions that you must take into consideration to come up with your pricing model & charges for your services.

Once again, refer to the worksheets provided to you in the ANNEXURE to help you as you begin to apply these principles.

THIS IS NOT THE END

The end is just the beginning. ~T.S. Eliot

From those that I have trained to become life coaches, I saw some common patterns within them:
- Overworked because of the demands placed by their boss(es)
- Tired of not having a life of their own
- Can't even get a leave or a vacation because their job "owns" them
- Plagued by uncertainty of the job market & environment
- Threatened by the climate of firing and lay-offs
- Some were already fired & tired of hunting for a job in an economy where employment rates are declining
- Unfulfilled and unhappy with the constant "politics" at work
- Searching for something more meaningful to do
- Most were thinking about quitting their job and starting their own life coaching business

- Some had already taken the plunge and were floundering and at the verge of giving up on their dreams.

If you have thought of quitting your job and starting your own business and still haven't done so yet, chances are that you are aware of the risks involved and have your own doubts and fears about it. You may be experiencing these:
- You don't know where to start
- You do not have any experience of starting/running a business or even selling anything
- Furthermore, you may not have anyone in your support network who has any experience with starting or running a business
- Possibly, you may not have a support network to rely on
- Possibly, your family might not be supportive of the idea of you jeopardizing their life for the sake of your fulfillment.

You need to realize, there is a cost to not doing your homework.

If you have no experience of starting or running a business if you don't even know where to start if you are unprepared......, then any resistance from your family and friends is totally justified because consider the research-backed statistics:

20% of businesses fail in the first year and another 13.33% fail in the second year. That means a total of

1/3rd of businesses fail in the first two crucial years, the main cause being lack of experience.

50% of businesses fail in five years

Only 33% of businesses survive after 10 years. This data takes into consideration a large variety of small businesses.

In my own personal experience, when it comes to the business of coaching and training, I have found that 90% of people (within the Indian context) who start a coaching/training business without any preparation of business, without any business planning, without any business strategy - end up going back to a job within 6 to 9 months.

Moreover, once they go back to a job, they forever sacrifice their dreams and aspirations and go back to a life of employment slavery, being unhappy, unfulfilled and disengaged.

The Key Is - To Be Prepared!

Getting ready to take the plunge from employment to business requires you to be prepared for the triad of - Psychology, Financial & Business.

Psychological Preparation
- Overcome not only your doubts but also provide the certainty to your family members that this will only improve the quality of your & their lives.

- Get used to the lack of a fixed but limited

monthly income in return for unfixed but potentially limitless income.

- Rid yourself of the reliance on a job for livelihood and develop your own ability to produce income on demand.

Financial Preparation
- Ready your finances for the swings that you can expect when you are in your own business.

- Apply financial principles that create the difference between business that thrive and those that barely survive or even fail.

- Financial success through developing financial acumen of business owners.

Business Preparation
- Design your business by learning about various business model patterns.

- Develop successful business strategies that fit your business design.

- Create time and financial freedom through developing business acumen.

I know that this book gives you a simple & easy way for you to get started; I also know that along the way you might need some help or additional inputs or support.

There is a lot more to pricing models, business models, client identification and setting up a business that generates profits and sets you free so that you have not only financial independence, but you also have a lot of freedom of time, freedom to choose who you work with as well as freedom to choose your purpose that you pursue with your work.

If you truly desire to pursue this freedom, you will have to do a lot more work. You will have to learn a lot more.

That is why I have created just the right platform where you can get this ongoing support & training so that you truly achieve the phenomenal success that you aspire for.

If you are interested to know more about this, all you need to do is go to my website (www.anildagia.com) and contact me to send your details and someone from my team will get back to you.

ANNEXURE WORKSHEETS

HOW TO GET COACHING CLIENTS – QUESTION WORKSHEET

Identify 1 or more groups of people that you would like to have as your clients based on their demographics like industry, profession, age, stage of life etc.

Hint – Find out about people whom you are already connected with in your social circle, in your professional circles, over social media platforms like linkedin, facebook etc.

_____

_____

_____

_____

_____

_____

_____

_____

_____

Identify individuals with whom you would like to establish contact & schedule a meeting. Ask for & setup a meeting.

During the meeting, seek to explore & understand what this persons dreams, goals & desires are & what problems/challenges this person faces, worries about the most and fears the most.

Hint – Take time to establish rapport, connect with them at an intellectual as well as emotional level. While the questions need to be answered, find your own way to seek answers to these questions. Sometimes people will answer if you ask them directly. Many times, they will get wary of you & suspicious and you may need to find this information indirectly.

Prepare a write up on how your services provide value to this person, how your services solve their challenge or problem, how your services benefit them so that they can get the result they desire.

Make it a point to communicate these points across to this individual in a subsequent meeting.

_____

_____

_____

_____

_____

_____

_____

_____

_____

_____

_____

_____

In that subsequent meeting – ask them directly, whether they would be interested in availing of your services and pay you for the value that you provide.

If they say no, or if they seem hesitant, ask them what more would they need to make a commitment to avail your services. Write down this answer. Assure them that you are asking this question only to improve the value perception of your services and not to force them to commit.

_____

_____

_____

_____

_____

_____

_____

_____

_____

_____

_____

HOW TO FIND YOUR NICHE – WORKSHEET

Total Number of PHENOMENALLY SUCCESSFUL coaching sessions = _____

Hint – The greater this number, greater will be the chance of you finding your niche. I recommend that you have this count as 100 or more.

Breakdown By Groups
Group Name & Total number of successful coaching sessions for that group

1. _____
2. _____
3. _____
4. _____
5. _____
6. _____
7. _____
8. _____

Breakdown By Topic / Result Area
Topic & Total number of successful coaching sessions for that group

1. _____
2. _____
3. _____
4. _____
5. _____
6. _____
7. _____
8. _____

Which 3 areas jump out at you as the most appealing? Make this your short list.

_____

_____

_____

_____

_____

_____

Keep this short list away for 1 month.

Look at this list again after 1 month & write down how you feel about each area identified in your short list.

If you still feel strongly about any 1 or 2 continue pursuing more in that area.

If not, repeat this whole exercise after 3 months.

HOW TO DECIDE WHAT TO CHARGE – WORKSHEET

For the result that your client wants, find out answers to the following question which will help give you an idea of what is it worth for the client

1. Why do you want the result that you want? What's the purpose?

2. For how long have you wanted this result?

3. How does, not having this result, affect you? What are the negative consequences of not having the result?

4. How does not having this result affect your relationships, your health, your happiness / peace of mind?

5. How does not having this result affect your finances?

6. How much money have you already spent on trying to get this result and not being able to do so?

7. How much money will continue to be lost on account of not having this result?

8. What are the other related problems you face by not having this result?

For the problem/challenge that the client has been facing, find out answers to the following question which will help give you an idea of what is it worth for the client

1.   Why do you want to overcome the problem? What's the purpose?

2.   For how long have you had this problem?

3.   How does, having this problem, affect you? What are the negative consequences of having this problem?

4.   How does having this problem affect your relationships, your health, your happiness / peace of mind?

5.   How does having this problem affect your finances?

6.   How much money have you already spent on trying to solve this problem and not being able to do so?

7.   How much money will continue to be lost on account of having this problem?

8. What are the other related problems you face by not having this result?

Calculate Your Assured Income

Total assured annual income from your non coaching business (or job) – **(AI)** =_____

Total non assured annual income from your non coaching business (or job) – **(A)**= _____
Certainty in percentage of achieving this non assured income – **(B)** = _____
Project certain income from non assured income based on certainty percentage
(A) X (B) / 100 = (C) = _____

Total Annual Income –
(AI) + (C) = (TI) = _____

Average hours worked per day – **(D)** = _____
Average days worked per month – **(H)** = _____
Total months worked in a year – **(M)** = _____

Hourly income certain from non coaching business (or job) = **(TI) / (D) X (H) X (M)**

This must be the minimum amount you charge per coaching session of 1 hour if not more.

Also by Anil Dagia

So, You Think You Can Sell?

Scan this QR code and open your browser to buy this book.

Video Companion To "So, You Think You Can Sell?"

Watch my exclusive video companion to So, You Think You Can Sell for deeper insights and practical tips!

Scan this QR code (or send it to someone to scan) to attend this webinar.

0 to 100 Rapid Client Acceleration
12 Weeks rapid selling system mentoring program

Scan this QR code and open your browser to know more about this program.

How To Become A Profitably Thriving ICF Credentialed Coach

Unlock your potential and transform your passion into a thriving coaching career

Scan this QR code (or send it to someone to scan)

to buy this book.   to attend webinar

ANIL DAGIA

How To Quit Your Job, Follow Your Passion & Start Your Own Business
Break free from the golden cage of employment

Scan this QR code (or send it to someone to scan)

to buy this book.   to attend webinar

Change Your Mind & Create Your Reality Using NLP
Unlock the secret to creating your dream reality

Scan this QR code (or send it to someone to scan)

to buy this book. to attend webinar

Chaotic Sales To Perfect Sales Machine
How to Build a Predictable, Automated System That Closes Deals for You

Scan this QR code (or send it to someone to scan)

to buy this book.   to attend webinar

Emotional Fitness Gym®
Beyond Emotional Intelligence

Scan this QR code (or send it to someone to scan) to buy this book.

My Book Of Quotes
My personal quotes to reflect on

Scan this QR code (or send it to someone to scan) to buy this book.

Learners Library
A living library where you can borrow a human

Scan this QR code (or send it to someone to scan) to subscribe.

HOW TO GET COACHING CLIENTS

ABOUT THE AUTHOR

Anil Dagia has been in the area of coaching & personal transformation for over a decade & has trained/coached over 250,000 people from across 19 nationalities including but not limited to Americans, Australians, British, Canadians, Dutch, Egyptians, French, German, Spanish, South Africans & many more.

He started by specializing in Neuro Linguistic Programming & over the course of his journey has incorporated the best practices from coaching, behavioral economics, psycho linguistics, philosophy, mainstream psychology, neuroscience & many more advanced methodologies & fields of study. He has even created his own model of transformation called Emotional Fitness Gym® .

In 2011, he quit his lucrative, cushy & high paying, successful career of IT to get into the profession of training and coaching. Since then, he became one of the top NLP trainers in the world. He gained a global trendsetter status when he became the 1st NLP trainer in the world to get an NLP certification training to be approved by International Coach Federation (ICF) for life coach certification training.

After quitting his employment, he realized that it is not only possible, but it's very fulfilling to earn an income of several 10s of lakhs along with being able to touch the lives of 10s of 1000s of people. He now teaches his students to become life coaches and earn an income in lakhs, even 10s of lakhs in a short span of time.

www.ingramcontent.com/pod-product-compliance
Lightning Source LLC
Chambersburg PA
CBHW020454220526
45464CB00002B/989